MW00512149

BLEED

BLEED

Poems

AARON PITRE

Aaron Pitre
www.aaronpitre.com

Printed in the United States of America
First Printing 2020
First Edition 2020

ISBN: 978-1-7359169-1-0

10 9 8 7 6 5 4 3 2 1

Library of Congress Cataloging-in-Publication Data
Pitre, Aaron
[Poems]
Bleed

For my husband, aunties, and cousins

Table of Contents

Bleed

I write

> *Pain*

These words

> *Grief*

To give

> *Anger*

The discomfort

> *Heartbreak*

That I've tried

> *Despair*

To abandon

> *Purge*

A seat at the table

> *Bleed.*

Before

There were six
years before
the shackles
rolled in
with the tide.

Five before
boots.

Four before
sneakers.

Three before
sandals.

Two before
socks.

And one

in which my feet

were bare.

I can't recall

the feeling

of sand

between ten

wet toes,

though I try.

The Child Knows

The child knows

toxic shame

the first time

the parent

hurts them

intentionally.

They might not

remember the

exact date, time,

or location,

but

the child

imagines-

no.

The child *knows*

that they

must be

the reason

for the wrath, thus

perpetuating the

cycle of self-hatred

with bulging eyes,

hot hands,

cold shoulders,

and screams. From

then on, the child

expects-

no.

The child *knows*

that the pain will

be just as

raw

the next time

as it was/will be

the last time,

though they'll

never know when

the next or last time

was/will be.

Confused and afraid,

the child believes-

no.

The child *knows*

that they will have to

learn how to

bend and break their

own will before

their parents,

  their world

then others,

  the world

do it for them.

Ill-equipped

to cope,

the child suspects-

no.

The child *knows*

that they

must find a way to

detach

from the body, so

they won't have to

feel

the blisters

or see

the bruises forming

just underneath

the top layer

of their thin,

uncomfortable skin.

Where ice,

kisses,

and band-aids

cannot reach.

Battery

the power of the man

who vowed to

protect me

has switched from

on

to

off

he

standing idly by

charging his battery

while the batterer charges

at me

my trembling knees

tell me

that my power is running out

so to keep

from dying

I'll suspend my mind

not speaking a word—

…

…

…

…

—'til I've found

an outlet

Cognitive Dissonance

Through the persistence

of abuse, my thoughts

have been edited

for family audiences.

My sense of normalcy dubbed

debaucherous in black bars

and pixelated images.

Had I not learned how to

access the original copy,

I would have watched

the pay-per-view perversion of

my life until my death,

fully confident

that it was supposed to

look, sound, and feel like this...

Inner Critic

I've only got
~~15 seconds~~
~~10 seconds~~
~~5 seconds~~

a moment of

~~freedom~~
~~confidence~~
~~calm~~

grace
before he
steps in to

~~change~~
~~edit~~
~~modify~~

pick apart
everything that I've

~~attempted~~
~~worked~~
~~struggled~~

pushed myself
to say.

Bubblicious Beings

it has

become apparent

to me

that my

flesh is

made of

bubble gum

and my

strawberry scented skin

does not

become

a man

but I like

the way

I

smell and taste

and it

terrifies me

to confess

that if

given a chance

I

think I might

like to

smell and taste

a

strawberry scented

bubblicious being

like me

Why Didn't I Run into the Rainbow?

A field trip

ended in a car accident

when my school bus

dropped me

head first

into my first pride parade

at half past 13.

Why didn't I run?

I saw

men kissing where

adolescent passengers

were hissing,

and on every

twisted lip,

I heard the far-off cry

of a me

that couldn't yet

be.

Why didn't I run?

Big Bird

whizzed by my window on

robin's egg roller skates,

wearing nothing more

than a ruby,

sequined jockstrap,

tangerine knee-highs,

and an indigo smile.

Why didn't I run?

His feathery

yellow buns

did a hot pink disco

punctuated with

violet twirls

that called my

emerald heart to

electric slide.

Why didn't I run

into the rainbow?

Grande jeté

with perfectly

pointed toes

into the orchestra

of color and light?

Moonwalk

in the champagne glow

of the sun

just after a storm?

When the air smells

like freedom

and the legendary

pot of gold appears

just outside the doors?

Do Not Call It the Gay 90s

In this time

which they do not call

the gay 90s,

I've been told my parts are

incompatible with skorts

and dookie braids.

So, I remain stuck

in buzz cuts and pants

with itchy tags

that read

"Made in the USA."

Le Harm

For Langston Hughes

It sags

Just like a heavy dream.

Like meat in sugar

Or a sore,

Or a sweet and over-rotten raisin.

Does it stink up the sun?

Run

Like a syrupy load

Deferred to dry like a crust

Or fester and then explode.

Does it like what happens?

Maybe it does…

Superficiality

If the space

between words

indicate

the hot air

at the source,

"I love you"

will hit

the ears

but miss

the heart.

The Dark Side of the Sun

I have seen you on Friday.
Felt your heat on my face
where a garden of freckles
planted with ninety-nine kisses
grew.

I have bathed in your light on Saturday-
a new shade for every hour.
Brick brown,
burnt umber
and best of all,
onyx. Addicted
to the smell of cinnamon on
my skin. Obsessed
with the dream of obsidian.
And if it weren't for the
flecks of ebony peeling
from my shoulder blades,
I certainly would have lingered

forever.

I have launched myself into outer space on Sunday,
taking off on sheer willpower
and determination desperate
to touch you;
the truest form of light
beyond the blues. Hoping
that with enough determination and
close enough proximity you
would reach out to
smother me in
your rays unlearning me
the definition of cold
in your embrace.

But what I did instead,
was pierce
      the veil,
penetrate
      your defenses,
and steal

your magic
by becoming earth-less.

Far too high
and way too mighty,
I discovered an endless night on Monday.
Swallowing the stars
by the millions, slowly
swallowing you
who, all along,
was nothing more
than a small
white
ball.
Glowing
but never shining.
Burning
but never warm.

Hand-Me-Down Love

I've resigned myself to watch
families reunited on TV
for an emotional contact high.

Living vicariously
through streaming tears
from a long-lost child
on ABC News
to a newfound parent
on Netflix.

Since I cannot get
a firsthand account,
a second hand satisfaction
will have to do.

I'd be lying
if I said that I wasn't

already accustomed

to the feeling of

hand-me-down love.

Tattered hugs and kisses

meant for someone else.

Them

Them.

Them

I hate

Them

I love

Them

No hate-d?

Them

Or was it love-d?

Them

I struggle to remember

Them

bit by bit

Them

    bite by bite

Them

    slowly

Them

    desperate

Them

    determined

Them

    to forget

Them.

Them

    holding the broom

Them

    I sweep

Them

    from the dark

Them

    corners of my mind

Them

    painful yesterdays

Them

    sad todays

Them

    sleepless nights

Them

    anxious tomorrows

Until

Them

    is
        all

Them

The

Th

T

...

No Strings Attached

I would like,

after thorough

investigation,

for some things

that seem too good

to be true

to be, in fact,

true

and good too. And

where strings were

supposed to attach

themselves, I would

love

to see

two violets

in bloom.

Love by Narcissus

It's a sad thing

to be the mirror

image of one

who only comes to you

when he wants to see

himself

and even more

painful to discover

in his reflection,

a hollow gesture

behind every loving act.

Take That

Take that hope
dash it.

Take that dream
smash it.

Take that word
violate it.

Take that wish
annihilate it.

Take that faith
crush it.

Take that tooth
brush it.

Take that love
fake it.

Take that promise
break it.

Take that time
waste it.

Take that bitterness
taste it.

Take that voice
raise it.

Take that abuse
praise it.

Take that gas
light it.

Take that truth
fight it.

Take that mind
lose it.

Take that path
choose it.

Take that kindness
shun it.

Take that scam
run it.

Take that money
spend it.

Take that start
end it.

Take that mouth
shut it.

Take that bullshit
cut it.

Take that life
quit it.

Take that road
hit it.

A Half-Life

To keep myself safe,

I've learned to blur the lines

around an identity

prohibited from fully forming.

Half of me repeatedly

under the influence,

seized until I learned

to give it away

for free.

      Or what I thought

               was love.

Half empty,

drained by thieves

who absolve themselves

of the crime

with toxic positivity.

My perpetrators declare me

"half full" and

"not half bad,"

     which when you think about it,

     is also not half good

     and thus pretty bad.

My other half has returned,

but there are no refunds

(or even a lost and found)

for the time lost

during my half life.

At best,

I can take the half life

that I have left

and start completely over,

learning how to be whole

in this world.

Lonely Tears

My lonely

tears have

turned to glue

on my face.

I tolerate

the stickiness,

but

cannot stand

the taste.

We Saw Thee Mark

For Paul Laurence Dunbar

We saw thee mark

Our bleeding cheeks

To pay the debt.

We saw thee mark

Our torn hearts

With human clay

To let our

Over-wise souls

See only Christ.

While counting

The myriad grins,

We saw thee mark

Our tortured hides and feet

With guile

But we let them smile.

Why?

We sing our sighs,
"But oh," and otherwise
In tears and subtleties.

We, the cries
Long and great
Arise from this world
But should we smile?
Nay.

O, thee be vile
The dream world that lies
And shades us all
Beneath it.

Memories of the Old Neighborhood

I remember

when luxury condos with balconies

were houses with names and color.

Grandmas-es and Bills-es

Aunt Fannie and the Twins-es;

cerulean, mint, and rose

with a cream trim.

I remember

the buttery scent of fresh-baked biscuits

sneaking out the house across the street

to hitch a ride down the block

on the shoulders of

carefree little kids

shredding the streets

on Big Wheels.

I remember

when the concrete parcels had grass

and blackberry bushes

that smelled like lilacs in spring,

and parking spaces

that were plum trees

in past lives.

I remember

the genus of belly laughter

that could only be found sitting

on a summer evening's stoop

when the mix of

barbecue, popsicles, and heat

was just right.

I remember

"ghetto gardening"

on lazy autumn afternoons,

tossing pinecones, cat tails,

holly berries, and figs

up high over a fence,

down a dark back alley,

certain that orchards would grow

if we planted the seeds before winter,

before the leaves were lost,

before the night overtook the day,

and the dirt turned to stone.

But most of all,

I remember

being safe and warm

inside my little old house,

just before sleep,

listening

to granddad's ghost stories

of Seneca Village,

the old West End,

and the ancient burial grounds

hidden beneath the city.

And I wonder,

as I lay me down,

if perhaps

that is where

the good old days

have gone to rest…

Race

For James Baldwin

Do they call it race

because we constantly have to run?

Outpacing danger

with our quick strides

so graceful

that they think we're dancing?

Or having fun?

Must we keep our steps twice as fast

just to come in dead last?

To dodge bullets

and booby traps?

To leap over hurdles,

the hounds on our heels,

and walls?

To protect our feet

when we shatter glass with our cleats?

Or merely to get half as far?

We have crossed
rivers and seas and centuries.
Shaped interstates with our footprints
from Blaine, Washington
to the Florida Keys.
When do we get to cross the finish line?

In a full-on sprint,
Baldwin asked
*"How much time do you want
for your progress?"*

Today,
around forty years later,
I ask
how much more
for a fraction of ours?

Soft & Sweet

Do I have to be smooth
to be seen as soft?

Sugar-coated
to be seen as sweet?

Must I always be
soft and sweet
to be seen
as safe?

Should I soften my edges
with a smile?

Sweeten my disposition
with apple pie?

Until at last,

I become detectable,

palatable, and harmless
to the eye?

Does the trick really work if
all it ever sees

is smooth and sugary?
Soft and sweet?

Ignorant and indifferent
to the substance underneath?

Coons

When we investigate
the exchange rate for
our souls putting up
our flesh and blood
as collateral for
monopoly money:
so do we become.

When we advocate the
slaughter of a native
son or daughter,
conflating place and time
with class and status
(none of which
are ever quite right):
so do we become.

When we hail the power
of quack medicine unproven

as protection from diseases
destroying our very bodies
while we proselytize fiction
and demonize fact:
so do we become.

When we believe
that the well wishes
of a particular ilk
will somehow alchemize
styrofoam and plastic wrap
into diamond and silk:
so do we become.

And when we get "rich"
on a dime
that could very well be
snatched back
at any time:
so do we become
        nothing more than...
            ...nonetheless

Sopo[o]r

What do you do

when the monsters

under the bed

take your toys

and threaten to shoot

if you ask

for their return?

You hide your anger

nicely

in the moth bites

on the ill-fitted sheets

they give you

to shield your

tawny skin.

You stifle your cries

neatly

in the broken

bits of elastic

that you tie

around your neck

in an attempt

to play the hero.

And you never

get to dream

because

the mattress padding

is thin and the

springs are rusty.

Because

the basement air

is muggy

and full of spores.

Because the night

always seems

to demand courage

and the day

never seems

to listen.

So, you find

a way to lie

down

still

to yourself,

forced to blur

the lines between

sleep

and apnea.

Intergenerationally Insecure

I have weak knees.
A gift from my mother
and her mother's mother
and her mother's
mother's mother
going all the way back to a grove
on the wrong side of the middle passage
where a great grand
as a young woman
fell from a poplar tree,
broke her neck
and died.

Her daughter
being a witness
became impregnated by the scene,

eventually bearing children

who bore children

who hate the color green

on autopilot.

I would like

to look upon

a fall grove in Mississippi

without fear

but I hate the sight.

In my

desperation to change,

I seek self-help in electronic gurus

who swear on sponsors

that a brain-body

without proper diet and exercise

becomes lazy

then weak

until it eventually finds itself

prejudiced

against the very thing it needs-

small changes

at a reasonable price.

But like all my

mama-ses neck-ses,

I been was broke

before I was born.

And if I'm honest,

I confess

that I'm accustomed

to the taste of pie

made with the

strange fruits

that too have fallen

from my family tree.

Flavors

that would surely disappear

if my taste buds change.

But I Don't See Color

Black bodies

beaten and bruised

black

and blue.

>*but I don't see color*

Black wo/mxn

broken and bleeding

black

and red.

>*but I don't see color*

White sheets

black blood

black

and white

and red all over.

>*but I don't see color*

Black blood

drawn by

blue men

who tell

white lies

red, white and blue.

but I don't see color

Can't breathe.

Seeing stars

and stripes

red and white.

Skin turning blue

red, white and blue.

Dizzy

and shaky

but still…

I don't see color.

I'm colorblind.

I can't even see

white

much less black

and without

breath

I can't even say

"color"

let alone

see

the color

of the knee

on my neck.

So, leave me

be

slowly fading

~~to black~~

~~to white~~

away.

Asphyxiating

as I see fit:

"colorblind"

without the "color-."

14 & 17 (2017)

When I was 14,

I wanted to be tall. I stood at 5 feet 6 inches; the same
height as Emmett.

I wanted to be a backup dancer for Janet Jackson.

I wanted the summer to pass quickly so I could finally start
high school.

When I was 17,

I found myself in the final week of shows of my first paying
job as an artist, in Seattle.

Then, I found myself in a strange land called "Connecticut"
getting paid to perform improv theatre, narrate educational
videos, dance at Bar Mitzvahs.

I could see that my dreams, big as they seemed, were not
impossible.

Oh, how I wanted to be 18, an adult, finally free to pursue
them.

Glad I got the chance…

Should I feel lucky? Should I feel "blessed?"

I'm tired of holding my breath as "cute" lil' black boys become black men, praying that they safely make the transition. And I'm sick of the "Well, maybe ifs…" that are freely qualified every time they don't.

Capital punishment for petty crimes.

The pettiest of all: Being black.

Emmett would be 75.

Trayvon would be 22. Today.

I'm 34, and I know that you don't care.

Your door is unlocked, but is it open? Do you still talk where you should listen?

Grandpa wears white sheets to dinner. Do you listen where you should talk?…

Pass the gravy, but don't say grace. Save your "thoughts and prayers" for yourself.

For Emmett, Trayvon, and all of us.

They Lynch Us Twice

They lynch us once

when they kill us

for spectator sport

by rope or bullet,

the medium matters

no more to them

than our stolen lives.

Our windpipes twisted

and crushed

under twine and leather.

Our mangled corpses,

riddled with shrapnel,

abandoned in the streets

to feed the vultures.

Then they hang us once more

by broadcasting our brutal murders,

unresolved, fetishized

and doomed to replay

over and over,

over our heads,

and in them,

for the rest of our lives

plus future generations,

all of which are spent

fighting for a justice

that never comes.

They lynch Lady Justice too,

hanging her along with

a so-called "jury of peers,"

but since she's made of marble,

and none of them is us,

she cannot feel our pain,

and they cannot give us justice

or life

for the life taken,

or peace

for the piece of us

taken with it.

We cannot rest

so, we stay woke,

forced to watch ourselves die,

twice lynched,

countless lives cut short,

the sirens warning us,

even when they're not for us,

to stay safe

but stay ready to be next

until we are (no justice)

either or... (no peace).

Of Thee I Sing

For Breonna Taylor, Elijah McClain, Tamir Rice,
George Floyd, Philando Castille, Atatiana Jefferson,
Eric Garner, Charleena Lyles, Alton Sterling,
Troy Davis, and George Junius Stinney

I sing of thee, the dead

in my dreams

of potential cut short

now residing limitless

in the astral plane

in radiant colors

the human

eye can't see.

I sing of thee, Breonna

in outer space

in the color "North Star"

in meteor showers

where out of the

corner of

my mind's eye,

I see you

moon-bathing

on Black Venus.

I sing of thee, Elijah

in the wind whistling

in the color "Concerto"

in harmonic breezes

that carve bouts

out of mahogany trees

and strings

from blades of grass.

I sing of thee, Tamir

in fire young and bright

in the color "reincarnation"

in molten heat

exploding from its

subterranean chambers

to shape

new islands

in Melanesia.

I sing of thee, George

in water gushing

in the color "Enough"

in the broken levies

sending the salt

of our souls

from the heavens

to the

ocean floor.

I sing of thee, Philando

in the earth bountiful

in the color "Innocence"

in the miraculously sweet

soil that

will train tomato vines

to grow

in wire cages.

I sing of thee, all

in the melody unfinished

in the color "Hoarse"

in the alto voice

that remains eternally at a

half-step beneath

the key.

I cannot stand the sound

but nonetheless I sing

of thee, Atatiana

to thee, Eric

of thee, Charleena and unborn child

to thee, Alton

of thee, Troy

to thee, little George Junius

I sing of thee, Mother Mercy

to thee, Father God…

For Us, We, You N'Em

For Us
never given nothing.

For We
who took that nothing
and turned it into something.

For You n'Em
always finding
new ways
outta no ways
to make
new somethings
outta new nothings.

Y'all been knew
can't nobody
tell us nothing
but

"Ain't we something?!"

Queer

Just as there is more
to a day
than sunrise and sunset,
more to the night
than dusk and dawn,
so are we nestled in
the hours between
and proudly out.

What scares people the most
is not the layered
expression of time
but rather the dissolution
it brings
of the meaning placed
on a construct
that is becoming
increasingly minute
by the second.

Having My Snack

We're not supposed to eat on the bus

      But I'ma have my snack.

A day-old donut, dry and hard in my grip

      But I'ma eat it.

It will become sand in my mouth

      But I'ma bite it.

Chomp.

This concrete cruller is damn-near scratching my tongue

      But I'ma keep chewin'.

My saliva is turning the crumbs to paste

      But I'ma keep tastin'.

A cloud of powdered sugar torches my esophagus

But I'ma still swallow.

Gulp.

My reddened eyes have flooded my face with tears
        But I'ma let 'em slide.

My lungs want to shit the crumb paste outta my throat
        But I'ma hold 'em down.

My shoulders are convulsing to the beat of closed-mouth
coughs
        But I'ma dance my dance.

My dysphonic "mmmm-MMMMMMMggghs" ring the
sound of death
        But I'ma sing my song.

"Are you okay?!" says the water-bottle-face-shoving
sistah to my right

But I'ma play it cool.

I'ma just

> nod
>
> accept her offer, gratefully
>
> take a sip…

Glug.

Then take another bite…

A Kinda Math (Alldisshit)

He

kinda black

plus He

kinda white too;

that makes

He

always get an interview, but

He

never get the job.

She

kinda light

plus She

kinda dark too;

that makes

She

seen by some, but

She

ignored by all.

Xe

kinda butch

plus Xe

kinda femme too;

that makes

Xe

get treated like a youngun, but

Xe

cleary ain't.

Dem

kinda boujee

plus Dem

kinda ghetto too;

that makes

Dem

exceptionally-excepted, but

Dem

still ruler-ruled.

Sumy'all

kinda city

plus Sumy'all

kinda country too;

that makes

Sumy'all

industrious, but

Sumy'all

stuck in fields.

Yer

kinda rich

plus Yer

kinda poor too;

that makes

Yer

livin' large, but

Yer

playin' house.

Ya
kinda nice
plus Ya
kinda mean too;
that makes
Ya
have comfort, but
Ya
need progress.

Tu
kinda hard
plus Tu
kinda soft too;
that makes Tu
talk loud, but
Tu
grieve on mute.

Webe

kinda dumb,

plus Webe

kinda smart too;

that makes

Webe

ready for the game, but

Webe

knowin' we can't win.

Summ'us

kinda angry

plus Summ'us kinda happy too;

that makes

Summ'us

get real hot, but

Summ'us

blame the weather.

Hellafolx

kinda passive

plus Hellafolx

kinda violent too;

that makes

Hellafolx

keep livin' today, but

Hellafolx

gon' die tomorrow.

Weez

kinda tired

plus Weez

kinda woke too;

that makes

Weez

feet hurt, but

Weez

taking care of you.

Alldisshit

kinda starts

plus Alldisshit

kinda stops too;

that makes

Alldisshit

confusing, but

I hope there's

some kinda pi(e/a)ce

in Alldisshit too.

Black, Regular, and Boring (BRB)

Do not consider it a special skill
to render color undetectable by phone
or ambiguous to the eyes.
Black is you still.

Taste buds that do not feature
fried chicken and watermelon,
earbuds that pin back
when rappers drop bars,
are not examples of refined tastes
elevated to a superhuman status.
Regular is you still.

A slave-free family tree
planted when we were kings and queens
by a five-times great grandpappy
in the ghetto-less heart of a hometown

where no one has ever experienced a single "ism"
does not warrant a call
to *Ripley's,* believe it or not.
Boring is you still.

Liberate the head stuck
in the chasm 'tween the cheeks
so that the eyes
(which do not see any better
in hazel, green, and blue)
may gaze
upon the self,
carved out of pride in abstinence
from behaviors labeled stereotypical,
and discover that the arrogant ass trapping it
ain't worth the number two
taken by any one of our gorgeous people
after Sunday dinner
has slapped the ribs
and settled in the gut.
Black, regular, and boring is you still.
As is you wonderful.

As is you divine

because you just as you is

is just

fine.

Ain't nothing wrong with

not being special

because special is not our duty to be,

especially when they take special,

hail it exceptional,

and rob us of the right to

just be.

If errbody "special in their own way,"

as the elders say we are,

then that would make "not special" exceptional,

and maybe that is why

you think you are.

But you are not,

which would not be bad at all

if you weren't trying so hard

to be different instead of just being

you

because uniquely black

is perfectly regular

is boring as hell

is freedom.

Dialectical Dissection

I dissected my dialect
beginning with an excavation of the vowels.
Unearthing the sweet tones,
which anthropologists have classified
as a Southern Black American subdivision
of the West African family.

Hidden within the consonants,
I found a formal structure
akin to a plantation home,
whose appearance
would not have been brought to life,
or made beautiful,
were it not for the black folk
who built and maintained it
for hundreds of years.

I found a washtub bass
interred in the vocal pitch,
producing notes of molasses,
buttery-deep and rich.

With a metal detector,
I combed the rhythms
on a rocky beach
where I dug up
ancient and priceless artifacts
much like those often stolen
from remnants of palaces
battered into ruins
and housed for profit
in museum mausoleums.

Thankfully, the rubble is composed
of large pieces
that I can reassemble,
with a bit of effort,
to create a new commonwealth of my own
where, in my king's speech,
which recounts my full journey
in a jazzy and poetic vernacular,
I'll celebrate what remains
of my mother tongue.

Grandmother Africa

I use

my imagination

to see you.

Shaping your face

in cookouts and film.

I claim you in my smile

and look for you in clues

scattered across the Atlantic.

Jambalaya in Jollof Rice,

Hot-Water Cornbread in Pâté,

Black-Eyed Peas in Akara,

which they say is Yoruba in origin.

I remember you in hymns

played on the marimba,

salsa dances, and brushstrokes

that seem to run muddy at the edges.

I tour old homes

where some claim you lived

as a queen in Senegal,

a warrior in Angola,

a textile merchant in Benin

in 1618.

I collect artifacts

to document my travels,

mainly masks that I put upon my face

to trace where the contours

line up like Africa and South America

when you put the two together.

I haven't found you yet

but I'm certain,

as we learn

to decolonize time

and technology,

that I will.

When I do,

I hope to gather my cousins

Saint Elizabeth, San Juan, e São Paulo,

in Louisiana y Havana,

Oaxaca et Fort-Liberté,

each to lay a bouquet

of jasmines at your feet.

Black Cat

Black cat,

up a tree,

wild and free,

I know you don't give a fuck.

Black cat,

you stay ready,

balanced and ever steady,

hopping trash cans to

fences and rooftops for

black joy.

Black cat,

they say you're bad luck,

just like your mother,

who they like to call a "witch,"

which they fancy a curse word

out of misogyny.

Black cat,

they cross the street

when they see you coming,

throw sticks and stones

because they don't understand

the meaning of black magic.

Black cat,

you is unbothered, though,

melanated all the way

down to your eyes,

black gold,

that never lose sight

of the way home,

no matter how far you go.

Black cat,

you is tough.

Thank god you have nine lives,

all of which

matter.

If it weren't for strays

of the bullet-dog extraction

and speed demons

too afraid of the dark,

I think you might live

forever.

Run Me This

Skin

so brown and lovely that the sun,

head over heels in love with the shade,

wanna add extra hours to the day:

    run me this.

Hair

so wild and free,

whose kinks and curls,

unafraid to stand up and show out,

do not wear uniforms when they dance

to the syncopated rhythms they create:

    run me this.

Lips

so full and big

they house a thousand hearts

sure to melt with a smile wide, a kiss juicy,

and room to spare:

> run me this.

Eyes

so dark and deep

they absorb starlight

every time they look to the heavens,

filling themselves with the rich mysteries

of the universe they reflect:

> run me this.

Noses

so wide and round,

built for taking in the open plain air

of the motherlands they still deem

"too primitive" to colonize:

> run me this.

African beauty

so black and pure,

whose majestic vistas span oceans in their entirety,

whose pristine nature we must protect

from those who seek to destroy it

for blood diamonds and ivory:

      run me this,

      all of this,

      and make it quick.

      The pulchritudinous all-that-ness

      plus a bag of barbecue chips-es.

      The is-ness that makes us anything but

      "ugly,"

      "not enough,"

      and "too much…"

I Exam

T H I S

is the distance transforming

Y O U

into the tiny letters that
barely recall what

W E

used to be and

I

recommend we get
new prescriptions

To: Little Old You

For as long
as I've known
little old you,
I've known
that a little bit
of little old you
goes a long way.

Today, I've learned
the hard way
that the long way,
in which a little bit
of little old you goes,
is now too far
for little old me.

Consequently,
I will suggest taking
the little bit
of little old you,

that has gone
the long way,
that now is too far,
a little bit farther.

Please go
a long way again,
but this time…
make sure the way
that little old you goes
is not only "too far"
but also "away."

Put the two together
then find a way
to stay that way
which I assure
little old you
will never ever be
too far away
to (and from)
little old me.

A Fighting Chance

Your daddy

doesn't like youinme

His daddy

didn't like himinim

It's hard for himinim

to even look at youinme

because youinme

remind himinim

of him

Your mommy

don't care about youinme

Her mama

didn't care about heriner

Heriner never wants to speak

to youinme because

all heriner ever hears

is her

Forgiving eyes

can see

that youinme is

neither himinem

nor him

An open heart

reveals

there's more

to hear

than heriner

and her

For example:

the sound of

a mirror

being inscribed

with the words

"I love you"

"I hear you"

in lipstick

One time

for himinim

and him

looking back

at youinme

Two time

for heriner

and her

looking forward

Affirmations

You...
~~ain't worth a shit~~
have value

They...
~~are better than you~~
have delusions

You are...
~~ugly, awkward, and stupid~~
fully human and beautiful

They are...
~~bigger, smarter, and wiser~~
inhumane and wholly
fragmented

You are worthy...
~~when they say so~~
~~when they like you~~
without question or restriction

They are lying...

about nothing

about some things

about everything, to create
conditions

You are worthy of…

nothing at all

table scraps

sloppy seconds

the delicious, radical decadence of self-care

They are lying to…

protect you

keep you humble

save your soul

preserve the faulty sense of a
self they secretly hate

You are worthy of love.

They are lying to you.

Failure

I failed today,

but in my failure,

I want to remember what I found:

a new sensation,

proudly seated in my heart's throne,

where shame sat since birth.

Last name: Satisfaction.

First name: Self.

They had a gentle smile

and sturdy legs.

Real Love

I grew a sugarcane

all by myself

in my garden.

Now that I've

tasted its nectar,

I realize

that every treat

I was given for

being a "good

boy" was

sweetened

artificially.

Healers by Chance

For the healers by chance,
when paths cross.

The anodyne delivered
in a friendly curbside smile.

The seed of self-esteem
in a gentle sidewalk nod.

The kind "hello" that warms the chest
and lingers on the tongue...

Gloria

For Gloria Toney Pitre

Gloria in drops of rain
which slip through our
hands cupped in prayer
before gently dissolving
into the ground

Laudimus te

Gloria in life
which cannot be lost
only deconstructed
into new ways of being
rooted in the soil
that holds the grains
risen in the voice that sings
"God Bless America"

Benedicimus te

Gloria in this
too-late hour which
brings forth new
understanding when
the moon is bright
enough
to trace our tears
and smile lines with
your light

Adoramus te

Gloria in excelsis Deo
for keeping you
eternally well.
And if said Deo
now is you,
Gloria in excelsis You
for bestowing upon us
the greatest gifts
a grand-mother
can give her *sweetsies:*

time and love

Glorificamus te

Gloria in the bounty
of wisdom harvested
in half a second
with the kiss on the cheek
that we miss most of all

In gloria Dei Matris

Amen.

Notes:

Laudimus te ("we praise you," Latin)
Benedicimus te ("we thank you," Latin)
Adoramus te ("we adore you," Latin)
Glorificamus te ("we glorify you," Latin)
Gloria in excelsis Deo ("glory in the highest to God," Latin)
In gloria Dei Matris ("in the glory of God the Mother," Latin)

Nostalgia

Sometimes,

I put on my favorite song

And as the music plays

The melody builds a vessel

That moves me through time

To an outer space

Deep within

Where I was restless and hungry

Small, green, and sweet

And for a moment

4 minutes 59 seconds to be exact...

My feelings smell like fresh-cut grass

And I'm overcome.

The Forgotten Ancestor

This is for the ancestor

who waits for you

alone

in the attic.

The little child

abandoned by time,

anticipating your return.

Spot them

keeping warm by the fire

behind your great-grandma's eyes

that skipped a few generations

to land on you.

Hear them

in the sound of soda bubbles

tickling your nose

when you claim the loudest belch

over your first cousin, twice removed.

Feel them
in the taste of
your grandfather's warm funnel cakes,
topped with
your great aunty's homemade peach ice cream.

Become them
when you're feeling free and stupid,
laughing yourself silly
for no reason at all
or crying yourself to sleep
when the world feels too grown.

Honor them
by speaking their name,
which was your name.
Let the sound invite
the pristine beauty and simple wisdom
of their innocence,

which was your innocence,

to come in.

Care for them

by letting them relax

in the soft caress of sun-drenched air

running free

in the meadow of your undivided attention.

Ask them

to come out and play

to take you by the hand

to roll, dance, run, skip, walk, limp and crawl

for as long you must

as long as you're moving

forward through life

together.

Blessed & Beautiful

My eyes have weakened
but they still bear witness to
many wonderful things.
Visual gifts
wrapped in my own delight in
the color violet
the Indian Ocean
paintings by Haring
Alvin Ailey dancers
I am clairvoyant.

My back aches
but at least I can
hear when it speaks
with each crack and
twinge loudly declaring
that I've lived fully
lifted my people up

carried the weight

in heavy times

I am strong.

My heart is broken

but the shattered pieces were

for a time

held together by a deep love.

Sweet taste of honey

worth every sting

I am fortunate.

And lucky

for now I have

new use for superglue

gold leaf

silver studs

and rhinestones now

blessed

with the knowledge

that when the pieces are

put back together

my heart will have

a newfound brilliance

I am beautiful.

I Wish to Live

For Lorraine Hansberry, Chadwick Boseman
Nina Simone, and Chi Chi DeVayne

I wish to live

fully in this dimension.

To experience

the beauty and goodness inherent

in being alive

as a child,

breathing and being

and being

being reason enough

to live.

I wish to love

from the pores of my skin

down to my pinky toe nails

expressing the precious dream

of a soul everlasting,

wide awake,

and curious to a smiling heart

gentle and kind.

I wish to taste the air
on Everest
touching heaven from the ground.
To canonize the distinct flavor
of the top of the world
in cookbooks and art.

I wish to witness the impossible.
To twerk on my strife 'til it
burns to ashes,
out of which a newborn phoenix
will rise through my sweaty smoke
to fly me to the outer arms
of the Milky Way.

I wish to be granted
the privilege of growing
from young,
gifted and black
to older,

brilliant and blacker,

be it luckily by years

or blessed

by just one breath more.

When the end feels near

with little breath left,

I wish to look back

at all that I wished for

in life and love

and give thanks

for the goodness that was granted

and the epiphany

that life and love are

the one-song that goes

on and on

and on

and on...

Revolution

Turn north.

Pull the seeds from yester eve's pain at midnight.

Turn east.

Root them deep beneath your feet at dawn.

Turn south.

Observe their wisdom flowering at noon.

Turn west.

Savor the honeyed essence of their fruits at dusk.

Turn north again.

As the fruits are rife with seeds fresh.

Keep turning.

For this is how you make a revolution…

About the Author

Aaron Pitre is from Seattle, Washington and is the author of the solo play *Inside the Cup*. A graduate of Suffolk University, *Bleed* is his debut poetry collection.

www.aaronpitre.com

CPSIA information can be obtained
at www.ICGtesting.com
Printed in the USA
BVHW061538250321
603414BV00003B/634